TALL TALE

by Natalie M. Rosinsky

Compass Point Books ✦ Minneapolis, Minnesota

Compass Point Books
3109 West 50th Street, #115
Minneapolis, MN 55410

Managing Editor: Catherine Neitge
Designer: ticktock Entertainment Ltd
Page Production: Bobbie Nuytten
Photo Researcher: Svetlana Zhurkin
Library Consultant: Kathleen Baxter

Art Director: Jaime Martens
Creative Director: Keith Griffin
Editorial Director: Nick Healy

Compass Point Books would like to acknowledge the contributions of Tish Farrell, who
authored earlier Write Your Own books and whose supporting text is reused in part herein.

Library of Congress Cataloging-in-Publication Data
Rosinsky, Natalie M. (Natalie Myra)
  Write your own tall tale / by Natalie M. Rosinsky.
     p. cm. — (Write your own)
  Includes bibliographical references and index.
  ISBN-13: 978-0-7565-3375-5 (library binding)
  ISBN-10: 0-7565-3375-9 (library binding)
  1. Folklore—Authorship. 2. Tall tales. I. Title. II. Series.
  GR44.5.R67 2008
  808'.0663982—dc22   2007012462

Visit Compass Point Books on the Internet at *www.compasspointbooks.com*
or e-mail your request to *custserv@compasspointbooks.com*

About the Author

Natalie M. Rosinsky is the award-winning author of
more than 100 works for young readers. She earned
graduate degrees from the University of Wisconsin-
Madison and has been a high school teacher and
college professor as well as a corporate trainer. Natalie,
who reads and writes in Mankato, Minnesota, says,
"My love of reading led me to write. I take pleasure in
framing ideas, crafting words, detailing other lives and
places. I am delighted to share these joys with young
authors in the Write Your Own series of books."

Have Enormous Fun

Tell a whopper of a tale, with humorous characters whose incredible adventures will leave you grinning. American tall tales are chock-full of heroes whose impossible exploits often explain the nation's landscape. Stories about such legendary figures as Paul Bunyan, John Henry, and Febold Feboldson are also tributes to the strength and quick thinking of America's pioneers. Some of these larger-than-life heroes are based on real people, while others were created totally out of the imaginations of people just like you.

You, too, can write your own tall tale. This book is the spade that will help you dig into your imagination. You will discover that you have ideas as big as the Grand Canyon and as funny as a six-toed snake! Read on for brainstorming and training activities to sharpen your writing skills. Tips and advice from famous writers and examples from their own work will also help you learn how to leave readers laughing.

CONTENTS

WANT TO BE A WRITER?

This book is the perfect place to start. It aims to give you the tools to write your own tall tale. Learn how to craft portraits of characters and plots with satisfying beginnings, middles, and endings. Examples from famous books appear throughout, with tips and techniques from published authors to help you on your way.

Get the writing habit

Do timed and regular practice. Real writers learn to write even when they don't particularly feel like it.

Create a tall tale-writing zone.

Keep a journal.

Carry a notebook—record interesting events and note how people behave and speak.

Generate ideas

Find a tall tale you want to tell or retell.

Think of a person whose story you want to tell.

Brainstorm to find out everything about your chosen tall tale.

Research settings, events, and people related to the tall tale.

| GETTING STARTED | SETTING THE SCENE | CHARACTERS | VIEWPOINT | SYNOPSES |

You can follow your progress by using the bar located on the bottom of each page. The orange color tells you how far along the tall tale writing process you have gotten. As the blocks are filled out, your tall tale will be growing.

Plan

What is your tall tale about?

What happens?

Plan beginning, middle, and end.

Write a synopsis or create storyboards.

Write

Write the first draft, then put it aside for a while.

Check spelling and dialogue —does it flow?

Remove unnecessary words.

Does the tall tale have a good title and satisfying ending?

Avoid clichés that do not suit your purpose.

Publish

Write or print the final draft.

Always keep a copy for yourself.

Send your tall tale to children's magazines, Internet writing sites, competitions, or school magazines.

AND PLOTS | WINNING WORDS | SCINTILLATING SPEECH | HINTS AND TIPS | THE NEXT STEP

When you get to the end of the bar, your book is ready to go! You are an author! You now need to decide what to do with your book and what your next project should be. Perhaps it will be a sequel to this tale, or maybe something completely different.

START YOUR TALL TALE ADVENTURE

What rib-tickling tales have already been told about good-natured giants who brag about their deeds? Are there female as well as male tall tale heroes? Find out by doing research in the library or on the Internet. When you sit down to write your tale, just like any writer you will need handy tools and a safe, comfortable place for your work. A computer can make writing quicker, but it is not essential. You can create chuckles even with simpler tools.

What you need

These materials will help you organize your ideas and your findings:

- small notebook that you carry everywhere
- paper for writing activities
- pencils or pens
- index cards for recording facts
- files or folders to keep your gathered information organized and safe
- dictionary, thesaurus, and encyclopedia

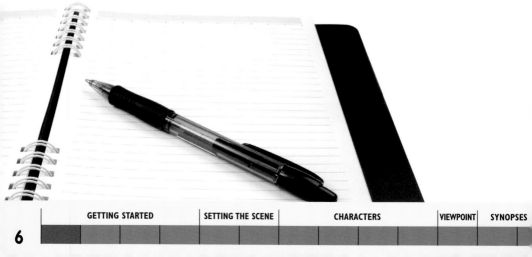

Find your writing place

Think about where you as a writer feel most comfortable and creative. Perhaps a spot in your bedroom works best for you. Possibly a corner in the public library is better. If your writing place is outside your home, store your writing materials in a take-along bag or backpack.

Create a tall tale-writing zone

- Play some of your favorite music or some folk music associated with tall tale heroes or settings.
- Use earplugs if you write best when it is quiet.
- Decorate your space with pictures of tall tale characters or of places associated with tall tales.
- Place objects that hold good memories from your own life around your space.

CASE STUDY

Sid Fleischman writes at home in his old-fashioned house on the California coast. He enjoys the sounds of the nearby Pacific Ocean as he works at a large table covered with books and research as well as pens, pencils, and a computer. Audrey Wood says, "When I need to write I do it no matter where I am or who's around me." This author has written on a bench, in bed, on a plane, and in a car.

Follow the writer's golden rule

Once you have chosen your writing space, go there regularly and often. It is all right to do other kinds of writing there—such as a diary or letters—as long as you *keep on writing!*

GET THE WRITING HABIT

Before you can write terrific tall tales, you have to build up your writing "muscles." Only tall tale heroes are born as strong as 20 horses! Just as an athlete lifts weights or a musician practices scales, you must train regularly. You cannot wait until you are in the mood or feel inspired.

Now it's your turn

That's a tall order!

Increase your knowledge. Look at collections of tales from the library or on the Internet. Examine tales from different parts of the United States. Find and read at least three tales that you have not heard of before.

In your writing place, use pen and paper to brainstorm about these and other tall tales. What do they have in common? What do you like most about them? Take 10 minutes to let your ideas gush freely onto the page like the tumbling waters of Niagara Falls. You may have just found the tall tale elements for your own story.

Tips and techniques

Set a regular amount of time and a schedule for your writing. It could be 10 minutes every morning before breakfast or one hour twice a week after supper. Then, come rain or shine, stick to your schedule.

CASE STUDY

Anne Isaacs wrote her original tall tale titled *Swamp Angel* after her daughter, then in second grade, complained to her. She said that girls in her school always had to make quilts during Pioneer Days, while boys got to choose activities. Isaacs says she thought about this unfair situation and imagined a woman in buckskin. According to Isaacs, this figure was "alive. She was real. She was Swamp Angel. Hands on hips, she said, 'Quiltin' is men's work!' in a Tennessee accent."

CASE STUDY

Mary Pope Osborne retells tales that say Paul Bunyan unknowingly created the Grand Canyon by dragging his huge pickax behind him. Captain Stormalong supposedly turned the Dover cliffs of England white when his huge, soapy ship squeezed between the cliffs and the coast of France. Pecos Bill supposedly created Death Valley when he fell out of the sky after lassoing and riding a tornado!

Now it's your turn

It's only natural!

Many tall tales explain how parts of the landscape—such as mountains, canyons, waterfalls, or deserts—began as the unintended results of a tall tale adventure. Look around and think back. What natural scenery in your area, or in places you have visited, is big and bold? Perhaps there is one special natural location—such as a large cave, meteor hole, or volcano—that you have always wanted to visit. Any of these natural spectacles could be the inspiration for your own tremendous tall tale.

Spend 10 minutes in your writing zone brainstorming what adventures might have led to the creation of that natural wonder. Scribble down all ideas as they come to you. Do not worry about grammar, spelling, or punctuation. Right now you are interested in the "big picture."

FIND YOUR VOICE

Being a good reader is a huge part of becoming a good writer. Reading will help you develop your writer's voice—a style of writing that is all your own. It takes lots of practice to acquire this unique voice. Writers continue to develop their voices throughout their lives. Skilled writers also learn to change their voices to match different subjects.

Finding your writer's voice

When you read as a writer, you notice the range and rhythm of different authors' words and sentences. Steven Kellogg and Virginia Hamilton capture the rhythms of everyday speech in different parts of the country, while Mary Pope Osborne begins her tale in a more formal way. Robert D. San Souci concentrates on detailed descriptions. Learning to recognize how different writers craft their stories is like learning to identify different types of music.

Experiment

You may usually read only funny or fantasy stories. Try other genres to see how authors of mystery or adventure, for instance, write with their own unique voices. You might get writing tips by reading about the adventures of Arthur Conan Doyle's famous detective Sherlock Holmes (right).

Writers' voices

Look at the words and sentences these writers use. Which writers use many adjectives and descriptions? Which writers use more formal language? Which writers use the rhythms of everyday speech in different parts of the country? Were these effective choices? Which style of writing do you prefer?

A legend grows about John Chapman, called Johnny Appleseed:
There's a ghost in the Ohio Valley. He moves over the windswept hills and through the apple orchards planted long ago. The farmers in the valley who've heard the ghost singing above the sound of the rustling trees call him by name—Johnny Appleseed.
Mary Pope Osborne, "Johnny Appleseed," in *American Tall Tales*

Mike Fink fights and learns to operate a keelboat:
After the orneriness had been squeezed out of Jack Carpenter, he became down-right agreeable. With Carpenter's help, Mike got the hang of navigating so quickly that the crew voted to make him captain.
Steven Kellogg, *Mike Fink: A Tall Tale*

A tale about Southern keelboat operator Annie Christmas:
Annie Christmas was coal black and tree tall. She stood seven feet barefoot, and she weighed two-ninety-nine pound. She would tell you she was the biggest woman in the state of Loo'siana, the strongest that ever lived in New Orleans-town. She was a keelboat operator up and down the Mississippi, and she knew New Orleans-town like the back of her hand. She dressed like a man, in harsh men's clothes. She had a mustache, too. She could make fists hard, and she would fight boatmen by the dozen and beat them down every time.
Virginia Hamilton, "Annie Christmas," in *Her Stories: African American Folktales, Fairy Tales, and True Tales*

Keelboat operator Sal Fink, daughter of Mike Fink, has an adventure:
Sal bided her time, letting her eyes slide from the grim, dirty, unshaven faces of the cutthroats to the pistols, knives, and daggers jammed in their broad belts. She thought that they were a pretty scruffy lot, with their filthy, red-and-black striped shirts, badly patched baggy trousers, and their beady eyes as bloodshot and red as the coarse red skullcaps they wore.
Robert D. San Souci, "Sal Fink," in *Cut From the Same Cloth*

GET YOUR FACTS STRAIGHT

Traditional tall tales often sprang from great challenges or changes that faced 19th-century Americans. Pioneers braved wild animals and traveled down dangerous rivers. Cowboys struggled through deserts and across prairies, while farmers battled drought, damaging storms, and insects. New technology threatened the livelihood of boat operators and railroad workers.

If you retell or create a new tall tale about such 19th-century heroes as Davy Crockett (left) or John Henry, get your facts straight. Use the library or Internet to learn what weapons or tools they used. Find out the names of the equipment Sal Fink or Annie Christmas would have used on their keelboats. What kind of crops would Febold Feboldson and his neighbors have grown in Nebraska? Make sure of your facts before you start exaggerating them.

Tips and techniques

Find a struggle going on now between people and technology in your community or elsewhere in the news. Perhaps this struggle involves losing jobs or fighting pollution. Use this news item in your own modern tall tale. Or use your feelings and ideas about this struggle to add life to your tale about an older tall tale hero.

CASE STUDY

Virginia Hamilton wrote that African-Americans told many tales about Annie Christmas, accepting her as a woman who actually lived. As these tall tales grew, she became a legendary character whose adventures and abilities are far beyond any real-life experience. Hamilton said we may never know for sure if Christmas was a real person, but stories about her remain exciting and important.

Similarly, tall tales about African-American railroad worker John Henry may be rooted in fact. Some people think that this larger-than-life character is based on a real African-American railroad worker who lived in Alabama or Mississippi. Whether or not "John Henry" actually lived, his struggle to defeat a pile-driving machine is a famous example of courage and determination.

A BIG COUNTRY AND BEYOND

Tall tales are told about every part of the United States. A few tall tale heroes cross borders and oceans. Two or three even have wild adventures that end up in outer space. Wherever you set your own tall tale, **your attention to detail will make its scenes come alive for readers. Even when a setting is exaggerated beyond real life, your imagination will help readers appreciate its strange, funny scenes.**

Sensational nature

Use as many of the five senses as you can to bring a scene to life. Mary Pope Osborne does this in her version of John Henry's contest with a mechanical pile driver:

> *Inside the dark tunnel, where the yellow dust and heat were so thick that most men would have smothered, John Henry hammered faster and faster. As clouds of stone dust billowed from the mouth of the tunnel, the crowd shouted and screamed. John Henry's hammers sounded like ten thousand hammers.*
>
> Mary Pope Osborne, "John Henry," in *American Tall Tales*

Readers can see, feel, and hear what is going on inside and near the railroad tunnel.

Now it's your turn

Be sensational!

Most tall tales have scenes set outdoors. Visit a natural setting with your writer's notebook in hand. Look around. Close your eyes and breathe deeply. Listen carefully. Run your hand through the grass or along a tree trunk. If it is winter, see how the snow or ice rests upon the earth and trees. Now take 10 minutes to jot down all the details your senses revealed. Use details like these as you describe scenes and events in your sensational tall tale.

Nature's wonders and disasters

Natural wonders are the settings of many tall tales. Paul Bunyan and his giant blue ox, Babe, supposedly created Minnesota's 10,000 lakes with their thundering, heavy footsteps.

Writer Audrey Wood in *The Bunyans* imagines the impact of an entire family of tall tale characters on the landscape.

She explains that Kentucky's Mammoth Cave resulted from the future Mrs. Bunyan digging to find a lost wishbone! Years later, according to this author, Paul Bunyan unintentionally created Niagara Falls when he scrubbed his dirty toddler in the Niagara River.

Both Pecos Bill and Anne Isaacs' Swamp Angel use their amazing strength and skill to lasso potentially disastrous tornadoes. Bill uses his lasso to fight another natural disaster—the worst drought Texas ever had:

> *It was so dry that all the rivers turned as powdery as biscuit flour. The parched grass was catching fire everywhere. For a while Bill and his gang managed to lasso water from the Rio Grande. When that river dried up, they lassoed water from the Gulf of Mexico.*
> Mary Pope Osborne, "Pecos Bill," in *American Tall Tales*

Tips and techniques
Do research in the library or on the Internet to see pictures or videos of natural wonders and disasters. Use your impressions of amazing caves, majestic mountains, or destructive storms as you vividly write the settings of your own tall tales.

The author's descriptive details bring this disaster to life so vividly that readers can accept its impossible solution with a smile.

Febold Feboldson also faces drought on the Nebraska prairie, but he uses cunning and far-fetched schemes rather than strength to solve this problem. Tales say he tricked frogs into croaking so loudly that they sounded like thunder. Supposedly, this thunder then drew real rain clouds to Nebraska. After that, according to writer Ariane Dewey, "It rained so hard that the frogs were washed down to the Gulf of Mexico. It took them nine months to hop back."

A whopper of a setting

Some tall tales heap one exaggeration upon another. Their silly settings are part of the fun. Readers soon realize that such tales are as much like real life as a circus act is. It is the writer's choice and job in such tales to provide whopping good entertainment from start to finish. Sid Fleischman does this when his original tall tale hero Josh McBroom describes his "wonderful one-acre farm":

> It's true—I did tell a lie once.
> I don't mean the summer nights we
> hung caged chickens in the farmhouse
> for lanterns. Those hens had eaten
> so many lightning bugs they glowed
> brighter'n kerosene lamps.
> And I don't mean the cold snap that came along so
> sudden that blazing sunshine froze to the ground.
> We pickaxed chunks of it for the stove to cook on.
> That's the genuine truth, sure and certain as my
> name's Josh McBroom.
> Sid Fleischman, *McBroom Tells a Lie*

Like Febold Feboldson, McBroom is a tall tale figure who overcomes challenges through his wits. His entertaining "whoppers" about his farm are part of the fun for readers. In this tale, we see how this clever character outwits a neighbor who thinks that he is smart enough to cheat McBroom.

McBroom's boasts about his farm are enjoyable because of the way he exaggerates and twists real facts. Lightning bugs do glow in the dark, and sunshine does give off heat—just not nearly enough to do what McBroom claims.

Tips and techniques
Twist and exaggerate real facts to make your own tall tale "whoppers" more enjoyable.

DISCOVER YOUR HERO

Will you retell or write a new tall tale for a traditional figure such as Paul Bunyan? Or will you create your own 19th-century or modern-day hero? Perhaps your tall tale hero—like Febold Feboldson or Josh McBroom—uses sly wit and humor as his "super powers." Most tall tale heroes, though, rely on their gigantic size and strength to meet challenges. They are born already big, brave, and boasting.

Tell your hero's problems

Tall tale heroes usually face problems right after they are born. They come equipped to tackle challenges, but those abilities themselves present problems. Alfred Bulltop Stormalong was born 18 feet tall! As Mary Pope Osborne notes, when this big baby smiled he also "let out a giant burp that nearly blew the roof off the meeting house." By the time he was 12, neighbors in Cape Cod, Massachusetts, send Stormalong away. They tell the sad boy, "The truth is, you've grown too big for this town. You can't fit in the schoolhouse, and you're too tall to work in a store." Baby Paul Bunyan has similar problems. When he was 9 months old, the 500-pound (225-kilogram) boy started to crawl and "caused an earthquake that shook the whole town" in Maine. His parents send him away, too.

Sally Ann Thunder Ann Whirlwind has an easier childhood in this version of her life:

> About two hundred years ago a remarkable infant came into the world, beaming like a sunrise. Having nine sons already, her parents were overjoyed to welcome their first daughter.
> "Howdy! I'm Sally Ann Thunder Ann Whirlwind!" shouted the baby in a voice as loud as a blast of buckshot.
> Her parents were astonished. "You can talk!" they cried.
> "I can out-talk, out-grin, out-scream, out-swim, and out-run any baby in Kentucky!" she announced.
> "You're amazing!" exclaimed her parents. Their sons, however, had been hoping for another brother, and they did not agree.
> Steven Kellogg, *Sally Ann Thunder Ann Whirlwind Crockett*

Sally Ann goes on to outdo her brothers and everyone else, have adventures, defeat giant beasts, and rescue and marry tall tale hero Davy Crockett. She never feels lonely or out of place as an adult—problems that do face gigantic Stormalong and Paul Bunyan.

Now it's your turn

Some gigantic headaches

If your tall tale hero is unusually big or strong, what problems does this character face as a baby? What problems occur as the character grows up? Brainstorm some of the gigantic headaches facing your hero. Draw six lines on a sheet of paper. Put one of these topics at the head of each column: Clothing, Home, School, Chores, Pets, Friends and Family, and Jobs. Take 10 to 15 minutes in your writing place to put at least two examples in every column. You now know at least 14 problems or difficulties facing your hero. You may use a few or several of these. They may lead you to still more ideas about your hero.

A SENSE OF HUMOR

Tall tale heroes face challenges with a sense of humor. Paul Robert Walker writes that Pecos Bill "chuckled to himself" right before he settles in to fight a mountain lion. He beats the mountain lion but instead of killing him, Bill saddles the creature and rides into an outlaw camp. Bill convinces the outlaws to join him as ranch hands, roaring "C'mon, boys! I got a little ranch I call New Mexico." Give your hero a friendly outlook and a sense of humor.

Find a good name

If you create an original tall tale hero, find a name or nickname bold enough to suit this character. It might suggest the setting of your tale. The Swamp Angel in Anne Isaacs' tale refers to the swamps in Tennessee. Because she shares her wealth with others, this character is as good as an angel. Similarly, Captain Stormalong is appropriate for a sailor hero who faces storms at sea.

Tips and techniques
Choose a name for your hero that reflects the character's actions and background.

CASE STUDY

Anne Isaacs first came across the phrase "swamp angel" in a dictionary of old-fashioned Americans words. She discovered and noted this unusual expression more than half a year before she began to think of writing a tall tale.

Give your hero weaknesses

The weaknesses of tall tale heroes have amazing consequences. By absentmindedly trailing his pickax behind him, Paul Bunyan carves the Grand Canyon. Many stories tell about heroes' plans not being fully thought through and having unexpected, fantastic results. In one Bunyan tale, the sun's heat pops a huge crop of corn. When Kansas cows see all that popped corn, they think they are in an icy snowstorm and freeze to death! For extra fun, give your hero a weakness such as being forgetful or clumsy. Or have the hero deal with unexpected and silly results from a complicated plan.

Now it's your turn

Larger-than-life characters

What qualities do you admire and find heroic? Look at individuals in your own life, read newspapers, or watch TV news to identify the actions of your personal heroes. Perhaps they are physically brave people, or perhaps you admire determination, honesty, loyalty, or quick thinking as much or more than physical daring. Use your own heroes to brainstorm the characters for your tall tale. While most tall tale heroes are super strong and physically brave, a few—like Febold Feboldson or Sid Fleischman's original character named McBroom—win mainly by their wits.

Keep these different types of heroes in mind as you brainstorm your own tall tale.

Take five minutes to list the qualities you admire. Now arrange this list to indicate which ones you value most. Use this list as you think up a storm of tall tale themes, plots, and characters.

CREATE YOUR VILLAIN

Your villain creates the problem or conflict facing the hero. In tall tales, this villain may not be a person at all. Many heroes fight wild animals or gigantic, silly versions of wild creatures. Sometimes a force of nature or natural disaster challenges the hero. Sometimes new technology is the foe. Even when human beings do oppose the hero, they usually end up as friends or associates. Villains who do not become friends are often greedy or ignorant rather than monstrously evil. Tall tales usually treat even villains in a lighthearted way.

Some tall tale villains

Silly or exaggerated versions of wild creatures:
Finally, Sally Ann flung herself into the King of the Mountain competition with such energy that she kicked up a tornado.
In a few seconds all the alligators had been blown away, and Sally Ann Thunder Ann Whirlwind Crockett stood alone as Queen of the Mountain. For the next few days it rained alligators from Minnesota to New Orleans.
Steven Kellogg, *Sally Ann Thunder Ann Whirlwind Crockett*

Forces of nature:
"What a place," Febold said to Eldad. "We're blown about by cyclones. We're frozen by blizzards. We're choked by dust. We're blinded by fog.
"There's no rain and the crops die. Or there's too much rain and the floods wash the crops away. If the floods don't get them, the grasshoppers do.
"But the weather can't beat me. It suits me fine."
Ariane Dewey, *Febold Feboldson*

New technology:
After the Civil War, steamships began to transport cargo over the seas. The days of the great sailing ships came to an end, and the courageous men who steered the beautiful Yankee clippers across the oceans also began to disappear. Mary Pope Osborne, "Stormalong," in *American Tall Tales*

Which kinds of villains will your tall tale hero face? Will your hero overcome them all? Or will new technology finally overtake this character's way of life—as it does to Captain Stormalong, Mike and Sal Fink, and John Henry?

Now it's your turn

A crazy critter!
Does your hero fight any crazy critters? In ancient myths, some monsters are combinations of animals. For example, in Greek myths a griffin has the head and wings of an eagle but the body of a lion. Other mythological monsters caused fear because they were extreme versions of animals. The hydra, for instance, had nine snaky heads.

Have fun brainstorming crazy critters your hero might defeat. In your writing place, take pen and paper in hand. Under the words "combinations" and "extreme versions," list at least five possible critters in each category. You may decide to use one or more of these creatures as a villain, or they may lead you to other new ideas for your tale.

DEVELOP A SUPPORTING CAST

You can tell readers much about your hero by showing how he or she interacts with other characters. Stretch your tall tale even further by developing a cast of characters that are funny or interesting in their own right.

Human relatives and acquaintances:

Some supporting characters display their personalities through phrases they repeat:

"Blow me down!" said the captain when Stormy stood before him.
"I've never seen a man as big as you before."
"I'm not a man," said Stormy. "I'm twelve years old."
"Blow me down again!" said the captain.
"I guess you'll have to be the biggest cabin boy in the world then. Welcome aboard, son."
Mary Pope Osborne, "Stormalong," in *American Tall Tales*

Unlike folks in Stormalong's hometown, the surprised captain is not threatened or worried by Stormalong's size. His amazed "Blow me down!" is the way he accepts and welcomes this young giant.

Unusual animals and wild creatures as friends:

In tall tales, animals as well as heroes can have amazing abilities:

Davy's best friend was a bear named Death Hug. While Davy
smoked his big bowl pipe in one corner of the cabin, Death Hug
smoked his small bowl pipe in the other corner.
Paul Robert Walker, "Davy Crockett Teaches the Steamboat
a Leetle Patriotism," in *Big Men, Big Country*

Later in this tale, Death Hug cuts a pair of boat paddles with his claws and uses his tail to help Davy Crockett steer a canoe.

Perhaps the most famous animal friend of a tall tale hero is Babe the Blue Ox:

> *Paul Bunyan and Babe the Blue Ox were inseparable after that. Babe grew so fast that Paul liked to close his eyes for a minute, count to ten, then look to see how much Babe had grown. Sometimes the ox would be a whole foot taller. It's a known fact that Babe's full-grown height was finally measured to be forty-two ax handles, and he weighed more than the combined weight of all the fish that ever got away.*
> Mary Pope Osborne, "Paul Bunyan," in *American Tall Tales*

Tips and techniques
Create interesting human and animal characters to interact with your tall tale hero. Tall tale animals are larger-than-life not only in size but deeds.

Tall tale heroes respect their extraordinary animal friends and expect other people to do so, too.

Have fun as you create unforgettable tall tale characters. Their strong, sincere feelings can be as refreshing as a tumble into a cold mountain stream on a hot summer day.

CHOOSE A POINT OF VIEW

Before you write the first incredible line of your tale, you must decide who is telling its story. Do you want readers to know all about the characters— what everyone is thinking, feeling,

and doing? Or do you want to follow the thoughts and experiences of just one character—such as your hero? Perhaps you have decided to retell a tale from the view-point of the villain or a minor character. These decisions determine your tall tale's point of view.

Omniscient viewpoint

Traditional tall tales are usually told from the all-seeing and all-knowing— the omniscient—point of view. The storyteller, or narrator, describes what all the characters think and feel and also shares knowledge of events beyond the characters' knowledge. Such tales often begin with the words "There was once." They often start just before or at the moment their extraordinary hero is born. The beginning of this tale about Davy Crockett is typical of this genre:

> *An extraordinary event once occurred in the land of Tennessee.*
> *A comet shot out of the sky like a ball of fox fire. But when the*
> *comet hit the top of a Tennessee mountain, a baby boy tumbled*
> *off and landed upright on his feet. His name was Davy Crockett.*
> Mary Pope Osborne, "Davy Crockett," in *American Tall Tales*

First-person viewpoint

The first-person viewpoint uses a character in the tale to narrate the story. This narrator uses words such as "I said" or "I thought" or "I did." Though it is an unusual choice for a tall tale, Sid Fleischman has lots of fun writing his McBroom stories from his hero's first-person viewpoint:

> *I don't intend to talk about it with a hee and a haw. Mercy, no! If you know me—Josh McBroom—you know I'd as soon live in a tree as tamper with the truth.*
> Sid Fleischman, "McBroom's Ear," in *McBroom's Wonderful One-Acre Farm*

McBroom tells events in a funny and suspenseful way. We want to know how he and his family will manage a grasshopper attack. His first-person account also creates a bit of mystery for readers. Why do McBroom and his wife keep feeding skinny Slim-Face Jim for supposedly doing chores they've already done themselves? Are the McBrooms being fooled? Or are they being kindhearted and generous? McBroom never reveals his thoughts here.

Third-person viewpoint

With the third-person viewpoint, the writer stays inside one character's mind but uses "he said" or "she thought" to describe events. This narrator can only tell what other characters think or feel through dialogue. Sometimes a writer switches between the omniscient and third-person viewpoints. Third-person viewpoint is often written in the past tense:

> *Pa Bunyan had an idea. He placed his daughter on Babe, and he led them to the Niagara River in Canada. The gargantuan father scooped out a huge hole in the middle of the riverbed. As the great river roared down into the deep hole, Teeny cried out in delight, "Niagara falls!" Teeny showered in the waterfall.*
> Audrey Wood, *The Bunyans*

CHAPTER 5: SYNOPSES AND PLOTS

TELL YOUR STORY'S STORY

As your tall tale takes shape like clothing sewed to fit its fantastic hero, it is a good idea to describe the tale in a paragraph or two. This is called a synopsis. If someone asked, "What is this tall tale about?" these paragraphs would be the answer. An editor often wants to see a synopsis of a story before accepting it for publication.

Study back and inside cover blurbs

Studying the information on the back or inside cover of a book— called the blurb—will help you write an effective synopsis. A good blurb contains a brief summary of a book's content. It also gives the tone of the book— whether it is serious or funny. Most important of all, the blurb makes readers want to open the book and read it cover-to-cover! That is certainly true of this blurb for Audrey Wood's book *The Bunyans*:

You may know that Paul Bunyan was taller than a redwood tree and stronger than fifty grizzly bears—but you may not know that he also had a wife and two children who helped him create some of the most striking natural wonders of North America.

With warmth, humor, and dazzling landscapes, award-winning writer Audrey Wood and acclaimed illustrator David Shannon team up to present the tall-tale beginnings of Niagara Falls, the Rocky Mountains, Old Faithful, and more. Meet the Bunyans—a family you'll never forget!

Now it's your turn

Announce it with flair

Write a blurb for the tall tale you plan to write. Summarizing the story in one or two paragraphs will sharpen your ideas.

Make a story map

One way to plan your tall tale is to think of it the way filmmakers prepare a movie. Before they start filming, they must know the main episodes that make up the story. They must also map out the plot (the sequence of events) in a series of sketches called storyboards. You can do this for your tall tale. The blurb you wrote will help you here.

Write a chapter synopsis

Another way to plan a longer work is to write a chapter synopsis. If your tall tale will be a chapter book, this method might help you tell it. You would group major events into four to eight categories. You would plan the plot of each category or chapter. Each chapter would have its own beginning, middle, and end. It would have the hero encountering a villain and facing a conflict.

BAIT THE HOOK

You have planned your plot, and you are now ready to capture your audience with your storytelling skills. What kind of "bait" will you use to reel in readers?

Different tall tale beginnings

If your tall tale hero is based on a real person, you might begin with an author's note explaining this. Mary Pope Osborne gives such information before she jumps in to her tales about Davy Crockett and Johnny Appleseed. Or your author's note might give information about your hero's way of life. In his introduction to *Mike Fink: A Tall Tale*, Steven Kellogg explains what keelboat operators did and how steamboats changed their lives.

After any introductions such as these, get ready to grab and hold on to your readers' attention. Be as bold as Pecos Bill and get out that storyteller's lasso!

Refer to your hero's unusual connections with animals:

> *Ask any coyote near the Pecos River in western Texas who was the best cowboy who ever lived, and he'll throw back his head and howl, "Ah-hooo!" If you didn't know already, that's coyote language for Pecos Bill.*
> Mary Pope Osborne, "Pecos Bill," in *American Tall Tales*

Tell a joke that uses tall tale exaggeration:

> *Mean? I don't know that our neighbor, Heck Jones, is the meanest man out here on the prairie, but for grab-all general cussedness he'll do. Take the time he stumbled into a patch of poison ivy. Do you think he got the all-over itches? Mercy, no! He gave those weeds a rash.*
> Sid Fleischman, *McBroom and the Great Race*

Begin right in the middle of the tale's most exciting event:

The tunnel was dark. Dirt and rocks were flying everywhere.
John Henry couldn't see. All he could hear was a terrible roar.
Sweat was dripping down his face, stinging his eyes.
Noise from the huge machine next to him was so loud it made his
teeth hurt. Of course, the heat was terrible, too. Steam covered John
like a hot, wet blanket. He felt like he was slowly roasting in an oven.
Bill Balcziak, *John Henry*

Set the extraordinary scene for the tale:

Back in the winter of the Blue Snow, the boys were logging
the giant pines of the North Woods. It was a pretty big
camp in those days, with a crew of 180 men. And
every man was at least seven feet tall
and weighed at least 350 pounds.
Paul Robert Walker, "Paul
Bunyan and the Winter
of the Blue Snow," in *Big
Men, Big Country*

Have fun figuring
out which way your
tall tale will round
up and corral readers!

Tips and techniques
Try out different openings for
your tale. Just as some varmints
escape a hero's grip at first,
your best opening may need
several attempts before
it is firmly in your grasp.

BUILD THE SUSPENSE

After your wonderful opening, you must not let your tall tale lose steam. Keep and build suspense for readers by showing the hero's lifetime of adventures.

Growing up … and up … and up!

Track your hero's amazing adventures year by year. Several tall tale writers have fun describing all the adventures that follow as young heroes enter each new stage in life. Tickle your own funny bone as well as readers' by creating astonishing deeds for an infant, a toddler, and an elementary school-age hero. Anne Isaacs does this for the Swamp Angel of her tale, Angelica Longrider:

Although her father gave her a shiny new ax to play with in the cradle, like any good Tennessee father would, she was a full two years old before she built her first log cabin.

… When she was twelve, a wagon train got mired in Dejection Swamp. The settlers had abandoned their covered wagons and nearly all hope besides. Suddenly, a young woman in a homespun dress tramped toward them out of the mists. She lifted those wagons like they were twigs in a puddle and set them on high ground.

"It's an angel!" cried the gape-mouthed pioneers.

Anne Isaacs, *Swamp Angel*

Steven Kellogg creates a similar history of Sally Ann Thunder Ann Whirlwind Crockett's growth:

> *Sally Ann continued to astonish folks throughout her childhood. When she was one year old, she beat the fastest runners in the state. At four she flipped the strongest arm wrestlers. At seven she was the champion tug-of-war team. On her eighth birthday Sally Ann decided she was grown-up and ready for new challenges. "I'm off to the frontier!" she announced.*
> Steven Kellogg, *Sally Ann Thunder Ann Whirlwind Crockett*

CASE STUDY

Steven Kellogg is an illustrator as well as an author. He created the drawings for all the tall tales he has written. Kellogg says that these pictures are one technique he uses "to advance the movement of the story." Another technique is planning when readers will need to turn the page to find out what happens next—"the element of surprise" in storytelling.

Larry Dane Brimner in his tall tale *Davy Crockett* has Davy starting life by riding into the world saddled to a streak of lightening. As readers learn of amazing feats, we begin to wonder about what marvels the hero will achieve when she or he is full-grown. This kind of tall tale "biography" is one good way to keep and build suspense.

A race against time

One way to keep readers on the edge of their seats is to place characters in a race against time. John Henry has only one workday to defeat the mechanical pile driver. As the day nears its end and he grows more and more weary, suspense builds. Readers wonder whether—despite his best efforts—John Henry will fail. In tales about Febold Feboldson and Josh McBroom, the heroes have to figure out ways to defeat plagues of insects before they eat everything in sight. Every minute counts in these races against time.

As tall tale heroes race from one adventure to the next, they supposedly invent new things and ways of life. These inventions reflect real changes that occurred in American society. Pecos Bill remarks in one tale that he has just invented the lasso. In another story, Paul Bunyan looks at the dark green forests, thinks of the pioneers' need for "houses, churches, ships, wagons, bridges, and barns," and says, "Babe, stand back. I'm about to invent logging." Another way to keep and build suspense in your tale is to include such exaggerated claims about "inventions." Readers will wonder what the next fantastic claim will be.

A gigantic battle

In a battle of tall tale heroes, who will win? In one of Steven Kellogg's tall tales, Mike Fink doubts that Sally Ann Thunder Ann Whirlwind Crockett really defeated those alligators. Fink sets out to scare the truth out of her. But he gets quite a surprise:

> *Folks knew that every strong man in the Mississippi Valley who wrestled the mighty Mike Fink found himself thrown flat, so they were amazed to hear that Mike had been flung five miles upriver by Sally Ann Thunder Ann Whirlwind Crockett.*
> Steven Kellogg, *Sally Ann Thunder Ann Whirlwind Crockett*

Another tall tale tells of a meeting between Davy Crockett and Mike Fink:

> *Mike Fink, feeling chock-full of fight himself, curved his neck and neighed like a horse.*
> *Davy Crockett thumped his chest and roared like a gorilla.*
> *Mike Fink threw back his head and howled like a wolf.*
> *Davy Crockett arched his back and screamed like a panther.*
> *The two of them kept carrying on— flapping, shaking, thumping, howling, screaming—until they both got too tired to carry on. Then Davy waved his hand. "Farewell, stranger. I'm satisfied now." "Me too," said Mike. "Feelin' much better myself."*
> Mary Pope Osborne, "Davy Crockett," in *American Tall Tales*

What would happen if two other tall tale heroes got into a brawl? What would happen if Davy Crockett and Mike Fink met again? Having your tall tale hero argue, try to outdo, or even fight another hero is one more way to keep and build suspense for the reader.

END WITH A BANG

Stories build up suspense until they reach a climax. After this dramatic point, the characters' main problems usually are solved. In many kinds of stories told about folk heroes, the hero has learned something, conquered an enemy, or earned a reward. Often everyone lives "happily ever after." This kind of ending is typical of many tall tales. Other tall tales, however, have endings that are more vague than this. After the climax, the fate of the larger-than-life hero remains mysterious and perhaps a bit unhappy. Often this mysterious ending is itself larger than life.

Conclude your adventure

What will happen to your tall tale hero after the climax of your tale? In Steven Kellogg's *Mike Fink: A Tall Tale*, young Mike Fink is "still cheered from one end of the river as the undefeated King of the Keelboatmen." This kind of happy ending is typical of tall tales that conclude during the middle of the hero's life. But it is not typical of another kind of tall tale. Tales of Pecos Bill's last adventure with his bride, Slue-foot Sue, fall into this other category. The pair end up in a surprising situation because of their stubbornness and super strength:

Together Pecos Bill and Slue-foot Sue bounced off the earth and went flying to the moon. And at that point Bill must have gotten some sort of foothold in a moon crater—because neither he nor Sue returned to earth. Not ever.
… When you hear a strange ah-hooing in the dark night, don't be fooled—that's the sound of Bill howling on the moon instead of at it. And when lights flash across the midnight sky, you can bet it's Bill and Sue riding the backs of some white-hot shooting stars.
Mary Pope Osborne, "Pecos Bill," in *American Tall Tales*

The fate of Pecos Bill and Slue-foot Sue is typical of this second type of tall tale ending. We do not know exactly what has happened to the hero, yet we believe that this figure, even after death, is still present in some way. Bill Balcziak's *John Henry* also concludes in this way. Other railroad workers were listening to "thunder from a faraway summer storm. They turned to each other and smiled. That sound, they said, was John Henry's mighty hammers pounding their eternal beat."

Tales about legendary Johnny Appleseed end on a similar note:

> *Other folks in the Ohio Valley still say that in the very early morning, before sunrise, if you go to a certain apple orchard at a bend in the river, you'll see smoke rising into the blue morning air. Johnny Appleseed is heating up his coffee over his fire. Soon his spirit will begin moving among the trees, waking the apple blossoms to a new day.*
> Mary Pope Osborne, "Johnny Appleseed," in *American Tall Tales*

Your tall tale might take place in the middle of your hero's life, long before all his or her adventures are over. In that case, a mysterious ending is not typical. But if you are writing the whole life story of a tall tale figure or writing about the hero's last adventures, you will want to consider adding mystery at the tail end of your tale.

Bad endings

To create a tall tale that leaves readers feeling as though they were 10 feet tall, avoid a bad ending. Bad endings are ones that:

- fizzle out or end abruptly because you've run out of ideas
- are too grim and depressing and leave readers with no hope

Now it's your turn

A grand ending

Reread the ending of one of your favorite tall tales. Could it have ended in another way? Write a new ending for this story. One way to write a new ending is to set the tale at a different point in the hero's life. Now put the stories aside. Go back later and read both versions of the tall tale. Which do you prefer—and why?

MAKE YOUR WORDS WORK

Your well-chosen words will work wonders. They will transport readers to tall tale territory, where heroes even change Earth's face. Every word counts. Just as a skillful logger or sailor does not use poor-quality tools, you must choose your words wisely. Only the most vivid and powerful words are worthy of your tale.

A sense of life

Use as many of the five senses as possible to make descriptions come alive. Sight, touch, and hearing help readers experience Paul Bunyan's rescue of young Babe from an unusual blizzard:

> *Paul fell asleep with his arm around the giant baby ox. He didn't know if the frozen babe would live or not. But when the morning sun began shining on the blue snow outside the cave, Paul felt a soft, wet nose nuzzling his neck. As the rough tongue licked his cheeks and nose and eyelids, Paul's joyous laughter shook the earth. He had found a friend.*
> Mary Pope Osborne, "Paul Bunyan," in *American Tall Tales*

CASE STUDY

Sid Fleischman says, "Imagery is a wonderful shorthand. ... Figures of speech are hard to think up at first, but they get easier."

Use vivid imagery

Use your imagination to create vivid word pictures with metaphors and similes. Paul Robert Walker uses metaphors to describe how an angry Davy Crockett leaves the steamboat to build his own wood canoe:

With Ben and Death Hug following, Davy stormed down the gangplank and into the forest. He found a hollow gum tree and chopped it down with a flash of lightning from his eyes.
Paul Robert Walker, "Davy Crockett Teaches the Steamboat a Leetle Patriotism," in *Big Men, Big Country*

This does not mean that Davy actually became a storm or that lightning really blazed from his eyes. These are word pictures that communicate how he moved angrily off the boat and how his eyes shone with this strong emotion.

In *Pecos Bill: A Tall Tale*, Steven Kellogg uses two similes to describe the appearance and behavior of a giant rattlesnake after Bill has fought it:

The snake squeezed hard, but Bill squeezed harder and he didn't let up until every drop of poison was out of that reptile, leaving it skinny as a rope and mild as a goldfish.
Steven Kellogg, *Pecos Bill: A Tall Tale*

These word pictures comparing the defeated snake to a rope and a goldfish help readers imagine its shape and attitude more vividly.

REALLY BIG COMPARISONS

Not surprisingly, tall tales use some really **BIG** comparisons. These exaggerated statements—called hyperbole—describe feelings and experiences through situations that could never happen in real life. They are bigger-than-life statements that match the larger-than-life nature and adventures of tall tale heroes. This description of Captain Stormalong's ship uses hyperbole several times:

The ship's towering masts had to be hinged to let the sun and the moon go by. The tips of the masts were padded so they wouldn't punch holes in the sky. The trip to the crow's nest took so long, the sailors who climbed to the top returned with gray beards. The vessel was so big that once, when she hit an island in the Caribbean Sea, she knocked it clear into the Gulf of Mexico!
Mary Pope Osborne, "Stormalong," in *American Tall Tales*

Of course, no ship could really be that big or move an island in that way.

Now it's your turn

That's incredible!

Reread a favorite tall tale and make note of the hyperbole in it. Now brainstorm some hyperbole about your own tall tale hero. In your writing place, have LOTS of fun finishing these statements with hyperbole. For example:

- My hero is as brave as a lion.
- My hero is so big that …
- My hero dares to …
- When my hero is determined, she …
- My hero once …
- When my hero was 2 years old, he …

Use hyperbole in your own tall tale to make it part of this grand storytelling tradition.

Write to excite

When you write action scenes, excite your readers with your word choice. Replace everyday action words with bold, unusual ones. Have characters race instead of run and leap instead of jump.

Tips and techniques

A metaphor describes something by calling it something else—for instance, a fierce man is a "tiger." A simile describes something by comparing it to something with the word "like" or "as." For example, a dewdrop sparkles like a diamond.

Steven Kellogg uses vivid action words along with a simile when describing how a steamboat challenged Mike Fink in his keelboat:

With whistles blowing, bells clanging, and smokestacks belching, the powerful steamboat charged forward like a rogue elephant.
Steven Kellogg, *Mike Fink: A Tall Tale*

Instead of *ringing* or *smoking*, Kellogg uses the more exciting words *clanging* and *belching*.

Now it's your turn

Take action!

By yourself or with a friend, make a list of 10 everyday action words such as walk or fly. Then have fun brainstorming at least four unusual substitutes for each word. Perhaps rocks would crash down a mountain instead of fall. A snake might slither instead of slide. Use a dictionary or thesaurus for extra help.

Remember—make every word count. Words will help you win and keep readers eager for your tales.

USE DRAMATIC DIALOGUE

Conversations can help readers understand people's personalities and relationships. Dialogue also gives readers' eyes a rest as it breaks up the page of narrative (storytelling). Done well, dialogue is a powerful storytelling tool—one that adds color and mood while it moves the plot forward.

Let your characters speak for themselves

One tall tale opens with Davy Crockett stuck in a tree. The conversation between Davy and a young woman who happens by reveals much about their personalities:

> *Just as he was about to give himself up for a goner, he heard a girl say,*
> *"What's the matter, stranger?"*
> *Even from his awkward position, he could see that she was extraordinary—*
> *tall as a hickory sapling, with arms as big as a keelboat tiller's.*
> *"My head's stuck, sweetie," he said. "And if you help me get it free, I'll give*
> *you a pretty little comb."*
> *"Don't call me sweetie," she said. "And don't worry about giving me no pretty*
> *little comb, neither. I'll free your old coconut, but just because I want to."*
> Mary Pope Osborne, "Sally Ann Thunder Ann Whirlwind," in
> *American Tall Tales*

Davy assumes that his female rescuer will be gentle and interested in ornaments. This sharp-tongued young woman, though, turns out to be a tall tale hero herself—Sally Ann Thunder Ann Whirlwind.

Hyperbole as self-talk

Like all tall tale heroes, Sally Ann Thunder Ann Whirlwind is far from shy. In a pattern of speech typical of these larger-than-life heroes, she uses colorful hyperbole as she boasts:

> I can tote a steamboat on my back, outscream a panther, and jump over my own shadow. I can double up crocodiles any day, and I like to wear a hornets' nest for my Sunday bonnet. … Furthermore, sweetie, I can blow out the moonlight and sing a wolf to sleep."
>
> Mary Pope Osborne, "Sally Ann Thunder Ann Whirlwind," in *American Tall Tales*

The difference between what Davy expects to hear and what Sally Ann says is funny. Davy is fascinated by Sally Ann's strength and confidence, and he finds out all he can about her adventures. By the end of this tale, he proposes marriage, and Sally Ann Thunder Ann Whirlwind accepts.

Tips and techniques

Your hero might be big, just like Paul Bunyan. Make sure your hero boasts in a BIG way. Be certain this character uses hyperbole to describe his or her own achievements and abilities.

FOLLOW CONVENTION

Dialogue is usually written down according to certain rules. Each new speaker begins a new paragraph. You already know that what a person actually said is enclosed in quotation marks, followed or preceded by a tag such as "he said" or "she said." Sometimes, to give the sense of a real conversation, writers place these tags in the middle of a sentence. This placement adds another rhythm to the conversation, making it more lifelike:

"To tell you the truth," said Chuck, "most Texans are flea-bitten outlaws, and the worst of them are the Hell's Gulch Gang."
Steven Kellogg, *Pecos Bill: A Tall Tale*

Tips and techniques
Use *say, said,* or *wrote* to introduce quotations. You can sometimes substitute words such as *complained, whispered,* or *shouted* for variety and when they suit the situation.

Now it's your turn

Listen in
Tune in to the way people talk. Turn on the radio or TV for 10 minutes, and copy down bits of conversation. Or jot down what you overhear on a train or bus or in an elevator or store. You will begin to notice how people often have favorite expressions and different rhythms to their speech. Sometimes someone may not wait to talk until the other person is finished. How can you use these different speech patterns in the dialogue you write?

More tall tale self-talk

Many tall tale heroes have unusual speech habits or favorite expressions. Sal Fink even acquired her nickname this way:

> In fact, she became known far and wide as the "Mississippi Screamer," because of the way she would bellow "Hi-i-i-i-i-ow-ow-ow-who-whooh!" when she was feeling high-spirited or ready for a fight.
> Robert D. San Souci, "Sal Fink," in *Cut From the Same Cloth*

The author has Sal use this yell throughout his tall tale about her.

In Steven Kellogg's tale, Mike Fink repeats the phrase "Cock-a-doodle-doo!" when he gets ready to fight. Sid Fleischman's hero Josh McBroom frequently *says* that he would never lie. McBroom also has the unusual habit of running all his many children's names together when he calls them. In Fleischman's tall tales, readers frequently see dialogue such as this:

> "Willjillhesterchesterpeterpollytimtommyl arryandlittleclarinda!" I called out. "After them, my lambs!"
> Sid Fleischman, *McBroom Tells a Lie*

Tips and techniques
Give your tall tale hero an unusual speech habit—a noise or a phrase that only that hero uses.

Now it's your turn

As she was saying …
Reread your tall tale. Are there parts of the narrative that could be better told in dialogue? Rewrite a scene using or adding dialogue. Now set both versions of the tale aside. Go back later and see which version you like more.

USE DIFFERENT VOICES

Writing dialogue is a challenge even for experienced, skilled writers. Remember that characters should not sound like you. How characters speak often reveals a great deal about their background.

A dialect of English:

Sally Ann Thunder Ann Whirlwind accepts a proposal using vocabulary and speech rhythms once typical in the southeastern United States:

> *"Oh, my stars and possum dogs, why not?" she said.*
> Mary Pope Osborne, "Sally Ann Thunder Ann Whirlwind,"
> in *American Tall Tales*

Dialect and educational background:

Sal Fink pronounces the words *for* and *certain* in a way that shows her regional background and limited education:

> *"Wake, snakes!" she yelled, in a voice loud enough to set the woods trembling, "The fat's in the fire fur sartin!"*
> Robert D. San Souci, "Sal Fink," in *Cut From the Same Cloth*

Another dialect:

Annie Christmas uses the rhythms and expressions of 19th-century African-American speech in Louisiana:

> *"I hope some big trouble gets you," she told the captain. "You'd better watch out this night. Your crew, too. For all that's bad is right with you!"*
> Virginia Hamilton, "Annie Christmas," in *Her Stories: African American Folktales, Fairy Tales, and True Tales*

Now it's your turn

Compress your dialogue

Try removing tags such as "he said" or "she shouted" from your dialogue. Does the pace of the conversation seem more natural? Does this pace better suit the mood and purpose of the scene? Can you still identify who is speaking? Some scenes work better with compressed dialogue that has no tags. If you cannot tell who is speaking without tags, you may want to work more to develop each character's voice.

Tips and techniques

Use speech patterns to clearly identify characters. Change the spelling of words to show any unusual pronunciation of words resulting from a character's unique background.

BEAT WRITER'S BLOCK

Even talented, professional writers sometimes deal with a troubling condition called writer's block. That is when a writer is stuck for words or ideas at the beginning or in the middle of a story. Do not fear. As a tall tale hero might say, "There are some surefire ways to tame that critter!"

Ignore your inner critic

Do not listen to that inner voice that might be whispering negative ideas about your writing. All writers experience some failures and rejection. Audrey Wood decided she wanted to be a writer in fourth grade. She began writing stories then but was not published until she was in her 20s.

Today Wood still expects to rewrite her work. After she finishes the draft of a story, she puts it away for "at least two or three days. When I come back to it," she says, "I have fresh eyes and … am able to see the strengths and flaws in my story that were invisible to me earlier. I often write up to 50 drafts of one manuscript."

Mary Pope Osborne also reassures young writers to expect to "rewrite, rewrite, rewrite." She says, "I like to tell kids that I'm never really hard on myself. If I write poorly, I don't get mad—I try to enjoy the process. I make it perfect by doing it over and over."

Now it's your turn

A character-building activity

Stuck in the middle of your story? Get to know your characters better. Ask yourself what makes a character angry, happy, or embarrassed. Then have this character write you a letter complaining about the story or other characters!

Tips and techniques
To get fresh ideas, take a break in a
different environment to think through
a writing problem. Or just take a break!

No ideas

If you have been follow-
ing the writer's golden rule
(writing regularly and often),
you already have a power-
ful weapon against writer's
block. Professional authors
fight and win this battle, too.

Sid Fleischman says,
"Some writers are fast.
Some of us are slow. Most
of us are both. Each new
book confronts the writer
with story problems he or
she may never have faced
before. … My tall tales about
the McBroom family, each
fifteen or so typed pages, take
me up to three months—that's gal-
loping for me. When I start a novel, I
know that I am going to be at the computer for the next year or so."

Fleischman believes "The problem
for the writer is not in finding ideas.
They are as common as weeds. What
to do with the idea that touches you
and excites your imagination—that's the writer's
problem." He once spent 18 months writing
just five pages of a picture book story titled *The
Whipping Boy*. Only after Fleishman figured out
that his tale better suited a novel was he able to
complete what became an award-winning book.

Tips and techniques
Make sure your story fits the genre
you have selected. Does your hero
belong in a historical or fantasy
story rather than a tall tale?

A WRITERS' GROUP

Writing may seem lonely. Some writers stomp down this loneliness by belonging to a writers' group. They meet regularly in person or over the Internet with "writing buddies." These critique groups help fight writer's

block by sharing ideas, experiences, and even goals. Or—like Audrey Wood, who often writes books with her husband, Don Wood—some writers share ideas with a family member or close friend. Mary Pope Osborne also sometimes works with her husband, Will Osborne, who acts and directs plays as well as writes.

Role play

Another way to beat loneliness as a writer is to involve your family or friends. Turn your writing problem into a game with them. Give each person a character role from your story, and see what ideas and dialogue turn up!

GETTING STARTED | SETTING THE SCENE | CHARACTERS | VIEWPOINT | SYNOPSES

Build character

Friends and family can help through another game. Sit in a circle. Write a character's name on a large sheet of paper, and describe this character to the other players. Pass the sheet around quickly, giving everyone just a minute or two to write down something about the character. This might be what the character looks like, thinks, used to do, or dreams. Keep going around the circle until you have 15 items written down. Then have fun reading these ideas aloud!

Now it's your turn

Stomp out writer's block with other writers!
Start a writers' group with other writers, or partner up with a writing buddy. Set a regular meeting time and place, and talk about how much new work you will bring to meetings.

NOW WHAT?

Congratulations!
Completing your own tall
tale is a huge achievement. You
have learned a lot about writing
and probably about yourself, too.
You are now ready to take the
next step in creating wonderful
new stories.

Another tall tale?

While writing this tall tale, you might have
had ideas for another one. Perhaps you
came across another tall tale hero whose
adventures you now want to tell. Perhaps
you want to write a tall tale set in modern
times, or a tale that explains the origin of a different natural
wonder. Perhaps you are interested in telling the events of your tall
tale from a different viewpoint. For example, how would members
of the Hell's Gulch Gang view the adventures of Pecos Bill?

How about a sequel?

Is there more to tell about the characters in your or someone else's completed tall tale? Perhaps a sequel will be your next writing project. How about a rematch between Mike Fink and Sally Ann Thunder Ann Whirlwind Crockett? What happened to the wife and son of John Henry?

Now it's your turn

Imagine that!

Brainstorm your next story with pen and paper. Think of a tall tale you enjoyed reading. List five things that might have happened to the hero or other characters after or even before the events described in the tale. Do not worry about punctuation or grammar as you jot down ideas. Repeat this process with another tall tale. When you are done, you may have found the characters and plot for your next writing project!

LEARN FROM THE AUTHORS

You can learn a great deal from the advice of successful writers. They know that someone who boasts about achieving success without hard work and occasional failure is just telling you a tall tale! Yet even though few writers earn enough from their books to make a living, they value their ability to create and communicate through written words.

Anne Isaacs

Anne Isaacs (left) was a shy child who loved to read. She did not start to write seriously until she was grown up and had her own children. She tells people who want to write, "Listening is important; so is reading. The more you play with words, the better. Share your stories or poems with friends and listen to what they have to say. … Do not give up. Above all, allow yourself to be surprised by what you put on the page; only then will it surprise your readers."

Steven Kellogg

As a kid, Steven Kellogg (above) made up and illustrated stories for his younger sisters. He majored in illustration in college and did some teaching after he graduated. Even though he had trained and planned for a career as an author/illustrator, Kellogg says, "It was an exciting moment when the first acceptances came in." Over the last 25 years, Kellogg has published more than 90 books. He realizes he is very lucky to be able to "tell stories on paper full time."

Sid Fleischman

Sid Fleischman first worked as a professional magician. He learned a lot about that job and about writing by reading books in the public library. He never planned to be a writer and only became interested in it after his own young children encouraged him.

Fleischman gave up on what became his award-winning book *The Whipping Boy* many times. His friend and fellow author Clyde Bulla always encouraged Fleischman to go back and tackle this project again.

PREPARE YOUR WORK

Let your tall tale rest in your desk drawer or on a shelf for several weeks. Then, when you read it through, you will have fresh eyes to spot any flaws.

Edit your work

Reading your work aloud is one way to make the writing crisper. Now is the time to check spelling and punctuation. When the tale is as good as it can be, write it out again or type it up on the computer. This is your manuscript.

Think of a title

Great titles capture the reader's interest. They not only indicate the subject of the book but also make the reader want to learn more about it. Paul Robert Walker's "Pecos Bill Finds a Ranch but Loses a Wife" is a more interesting title than "Meet Pecos Bill."

Be professional

If you have a computer, you can type up your manuscript to give it a professional presentation. Manuscripts should always be printed on one side of white paper, with wide margins and double spacing. Pages should be numbered, and new chapters should start on a new page. You should also include your title as a header on the top of each page. At the front, you should have a title page with your name, address, telephone number, and e-mail address on it.

Make your own book

If your school has its own computer lab, why not use it to publish your tall tale? A computer will let you choose your own font (print style) or justify the text (making margins even like a professionally printed page). When you have typed and saved the tall tale to a file, you can edit it quickly with the spelling and grammar checker, or move sections around using the cut-and-paste tool, which saves a lot of rewriting. A graphics program will let you design and print a cover for the book, too.

Having the tall tale on a computer file also means you can print a copy whenever you need one or revise the whole tale if you want to.

Tips and techniques
Always make a copy of your tall tale before you give it to others to read. Otherwise, if they lose it, you may have lost all your valuable work.

REACH YOUR AUDIENCE

The next step is to find an audience for your tale. Family members or classmates may be receptive. Members of a community group such as a Boy Scout troop or a senior citizens center might like to read your work. Or you may want to share your work through a Web site, a literary magazine, or a publishing house.

Places to publish your tall tale

There are several magazines and writing Web sites that accept tall tales from young authors. Some give writing advice and run regular competitions. Each site has its own rules about submitting work, so remember to read these carefully. Here are two more ideas:

- Send the tall tale to your school paper.
- Watch your local newspaper for writing competitions you could enter.

Finding a publisher

Study the market to find out which publishers publish tall tales. Addresses of publishers and information about whether they accept submissions can be found in writers' handbooks in your local library. Remember that manuscripts that haven't been asked for or paid for by a publisher are rarely published.

Getting it ready

Secure any submission you send with a staple or paper clip, and always enclose a short letter (explaining what you have sent) and a stamped, self-addressed envelope for the tale's return.

Writer's tip

Don't lose heart if an editor rejects your tall tale. See this as a chance to make your work better and try again. Remember, having your work published is wonderful, but it is not the only thing. Being able to write a tall tale is an accomplishment that will delight the people you love. Talk about it to your younger brother or sister. Read it to your grandfather. Find your audience.

Some final words

You are now a member of a great story-telling tradition. People across the United States have told tall tales for hundreds of years. You have shown that you too can write a tale that displays humor, imagination, a sense of adventure, and a talent for wild and wonderful exaggeration. With this success and knowledge, you are ready to set out on the next grand adventure in your life!

Read! Write!

And remember to think and dream big.

CHAPTER 10: FIND OUT MORE

Glossary

chapter synopsis—an outline that describes briefly what happens in each chapter

edit—to remove all unnecessary words from your story, correcting errors, and rewriting the text until the story is the best it can be

editor—the person at a publishing house who finds new books to publish and advises authors on how to improve their stories by telling them what needs to be added or cut

first-person viewpoint—a viewpoint that allows a single character to tell the story as if he or she had written it; readers feel as if that character is talking directly to them

genres—categories of writing characterized by a particular style, form, or content

hyperbole—(pronounced hi-PUR-buh-lee) a figure of speech that exaggerates on purpose, such as "I could sleep for a week"

manuscript—book or article typed or written by hand

metaphor—a figure of speech that paints a word picture; calling a man "a mouse" is a metaphor from which we learn in one word that the man is timid or weak, not that he is actually a mouse

narrative—the telling of a story

omniscient viewpoint—an all-seeing narrator who sees all the characters and tells readers how they are acting and feeling

plot—the sequence of events that drive a story forward; the problems that the hero must resolve

point of view—the eyes through which a story is told

publisher—a person or company who pays for an author's manuscript to be printed as a book and who distributes and sells that book

sequel—a story that carries an existing one forward

simile—saying something is like something else, a word picture, such as "clouds like frayed lace"

synopsis—a short summary that describes what a story is about and introduces the main characters

third-person viewpoint—a viewpoint that describes the events of the story through a single character's eyes

unsolicited manuscripts—manuscripts that are sent to publishers without being requested; these submissions usually end up in the "slush pile," where they may wait a long time to be read

writer's block—when writers think they can no longer write or have used up all their ideas

Further information

Visit your local libraries and make friends with the librarians. They can direct you to useful sources of information, including magazines that publish young people's short fiction. You can learn your craft and read great stories at the same time.

Librarians will also know if any published authors are scheduled to speak in your area. Many authors visit schools and offer writing workshops. Ask your teacher to invite a favorite author to speak at your school.

On the Web

For more information on this topic, use FactHound.

1. Go to www.facthound.com
2. Type in this book ID: 0756533759
3. Click on the *Fetch It* button.

FactHound will find the best Web sites for you.

Read all the Write Your Own books

Write Your Own Adventure Story
Write Your Own Biography
Write Your Own Fairy Tale
Write Your Own Fantasy Story
Write Your Own Historical Fiction Story
Write Your Own Mystery Story
Write Your Own Myth
Write Your Own Realistic Fiction Story
Write Your Own Science Fiction Story
Write Your Own Tall Tale

Read more tall tales

Balcziak, Bill. *Johnny Appleseed.* Minneapolis: Compass Point Books, 2003.

Balcziak, Bill. *Pecos Bill.* Minneapolis: Compass Point Books, 2003.

Bania, Michael. *Kumak's Fish: A Tall Tale from the Far North.* Portland, Ore.: Alaska Northwest Books, 2004.

Brimner, Larry Dane. *Captain Stormalong.* Minneapolis: Compass Point Books, 2004.

Fleischman, Sid. *McBroom's Ghost.* New York: Price Stern Sloan, 1998.

Glass, Andrew. *Mountain Men: True Grit and Tall Tales.* New York: Doubleday Books for Young Readers, 2001.

Hopkinson, Deborah. *Apples to Oregon.* New York: Atheneum Books for Young Readers, 2004.

Kellogg, Steven. *Johnny Appleseed: A Tall Tale.* New York: Morrow Junior Books, 1988.

Kellogg, Steven. *Paul Bunyan: A Tall Tale.* New York: W. Morrow, 1984.

Mason, Jane. *Paul Bunyan and Other Tall Tales.* New York: Scholastic, 2002.

Myers, Christopher. *Lies and Other Tall Tales; Collected by Zora Neale Hurston.* New York: HarperCollins, 2005.

Nolen, Jerdine. *Thunder Rose.* San Diego: Harcourt, 2003.

Shepard, Aaron. *Master Man: A Tall Tale of Nigeria.* New York: HarperCollins, 2001.

Thomassie, Tynia. *Feliciana Feydra LeRoux: A Cajun Tall Tale.* Boston: Little, Brown, 1995.

Thomassie, Tynia. *Feliciana Meets d'Loup Garou: A Cajun Tall Tale.* Boston: Little, Brown, 1998.

Books cited

Balcziak, Bill. *John Henry.* Minneapolis: Compass Point Books, 2003.

Brimner, Larry Dane. *Davy Crockett.* Minneapolis: Compass Point Books, 2004.

Dewey, Ariane. *Febold Feboldson.* New York: Greenwillow Books, 1984.

Fleischman, Sid. *McBroom and the Great Race.* Boston: Little, Brown, 1980.

Fleischman, Sid. *McBroom Tells a Lie.* Boston: Price Stern Sloan, 1999.

Fleischman, Sid. *McBroom's Wonderful One-Acre Farm: Three Tall Tales.* New York: Greenwillow Books, 1992.

Hamilton, Virginia. *Her Stories: African American Folktales, Fairy Tales, and True Tales.* New York: Blue Sky Press, 1995.

Isaacs, Anne. *Swamp Angel.* New York: Dutton Children's Books, 1994.

Kellogg, Steven. *Mike Fink: A Tall Tale.* New York: Morrow Junior Books, 1992.

Kellogg, Steven. *Pecos Bill: A Tall Tale.* New York: Morrow, 1986.

Kellogg, Steven. *Sally Ann Thunder Ann Whirlwind Crockett: A Tall Tale.* New York: Morrow Junior Books, 1995.

Osborne, Mary Pope. *American Tall Tales.* New York: Knopf, 1991.

San Souci, Robert D. *Cut From the Same Cloth: American Women of Myth, Legend, and Tall Tale.* New York: Philomel Books, 1993.

Walker, Paul Robert. *Big Men, Big Country: A Collection of American Tall Tales.* San Diego: Harcourt Brace Jovanovich, 1993.

Wood, Audrey. *The Bunyans.* New York: Blue Sky Press/Scholastic, 1996.

Image credits

Index